It's Easy To Play Nursery Rhymes.

Wise Publications
London/New York/Sydney

Exclusive Distributors:
Music Sales Limited
8/9 Frith Street, London W1V 5TZ
Music Sales Corporation
257 Park Avenue South, New York, N.Y. 10010, USA
Music Sales Pty. Limited
120 Rothschild Avenue, Roseberg, NSW 2018, Australia

This book © Copyright 1984 by
Wise Publications
ISBN 0.7119.0567.3
Order No. AM 37706

Art direction by Mike Bell
Cover illustration by Graham Percy
Arranged and compiled by Cyril Watters

Music Sales complete catalogue lists thousands of
titles and is free from your local music
book shop, or direct from Music Sales Limited.
Please send a cheque or Postal Order for £1.50 for postage to
Music Sales Limited, 8/9 Frith Street, London W1V 5TZ.

Unauthorised reproduction of any part
of this publication by any means including
photocopying is an infringement of copyright.

Printed in England by
Caligraving Limited, Thetford, Norfolk

Sing A Song Of Sixpence

Traditional

© Copyright 1984 Dorsey Brothers Music Limited, London W1.

Little Bo-Peep

Traditional

Fairly slow

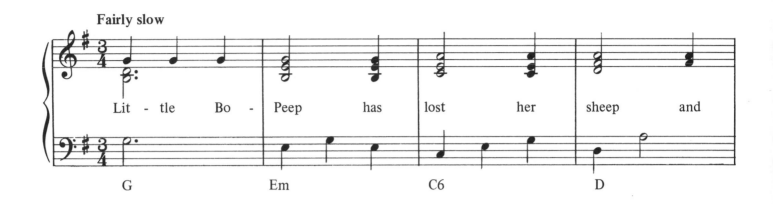

Lit - tle Bo - Peep has lost her sheep and

G   Em   C6   D

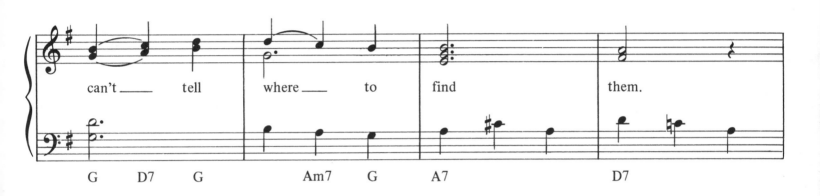

can't ___ tell where ___ to find them.

G D7 G   Am7 G A7   D7

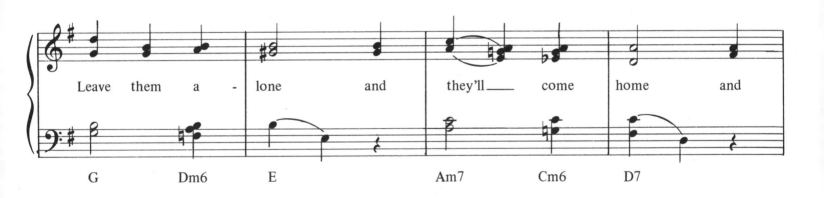

Leave them a - lone and they'll ___ come home and

G Dm6   E   Am7 Cm6 D7

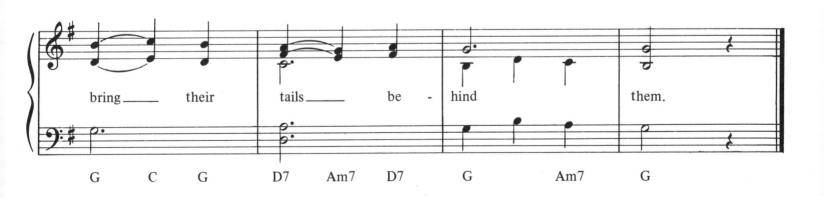

bring ___ their tails ___ be - hind them.

G C G   D7 Am7 D7   G Am7 G

© Copyright 1984 Dorsey Brothers Music Limited, London W1.

Tom Tom The Piper's Son

Traditional

Tom, Tom the pi-per's son, stole a pig and a-way he run; the

G   C   G   Em   Am7   D

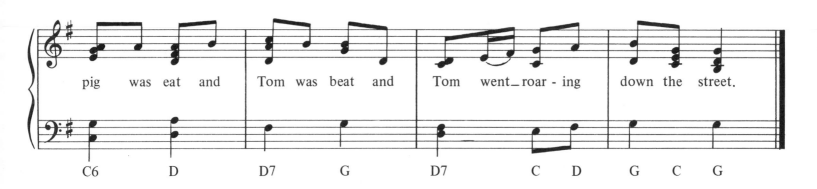

pig was eat and Tom was beat and Tom went—roar-ing down the street.

C6   D   D7   G   D7   C   D   G   C   G

© Copyright 1984 Dorsey Brothers Music Limited, London W1.

London Bridge Is Falling Down

Traditional

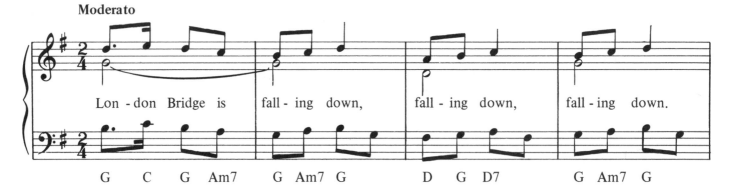

Lon-don Bridge is fall-ing down, fall-ing down, fall-ing down.

G   C   G   Am7   G   Am7   G   D   G   D7   G   Am7   G

Lon-don Bridge is fall-ing down, My fair la-dy.___

G   C   G   Am7   G   Am7   G   Am7   D7   G

© Copyright 1984 Dorsey Brothers Music Limited, London W1.

Yankee Doodle

Traditional

Moderato

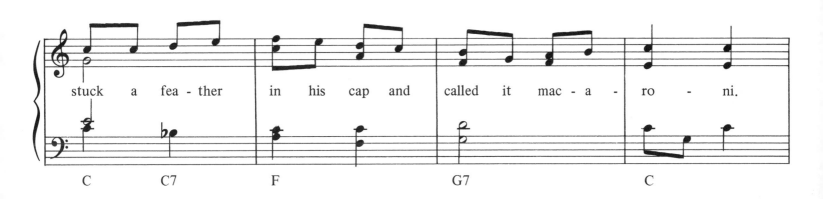

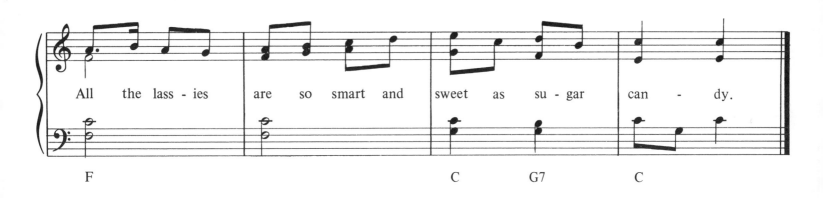

© Copyright 1984 Dorsey Brothers Music Limited, London W1.

7

Hush A Bye Baby

Traditional

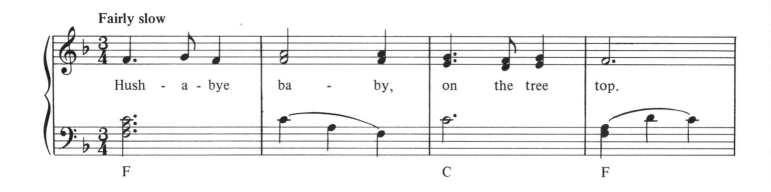

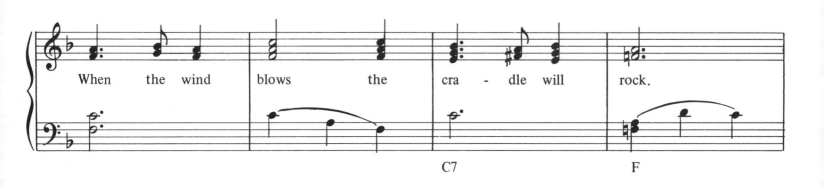

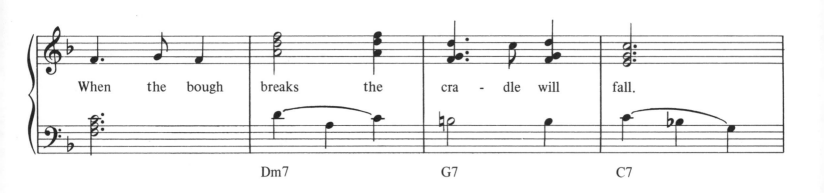

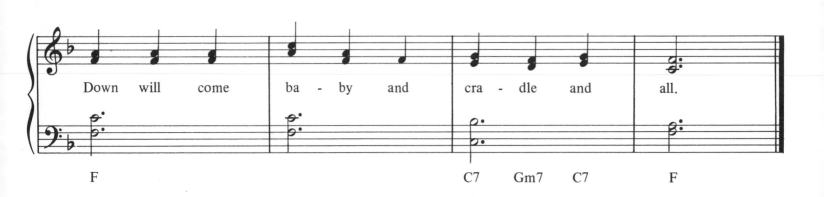

© Copyright 1984 Dorsey Brothers Music Limited, London W1.

Pop Goes The Weasel

Traditional

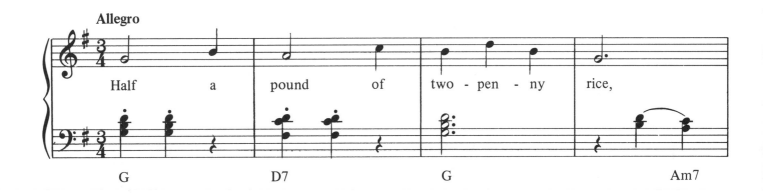

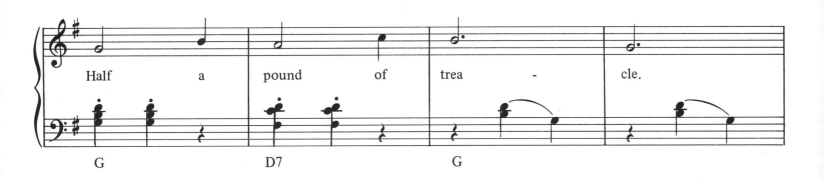

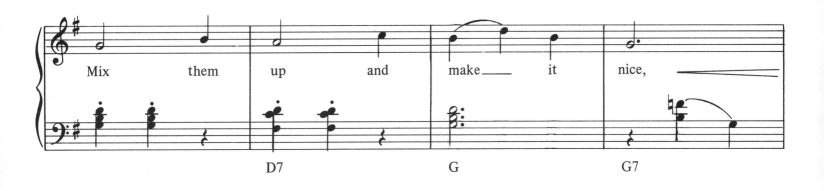

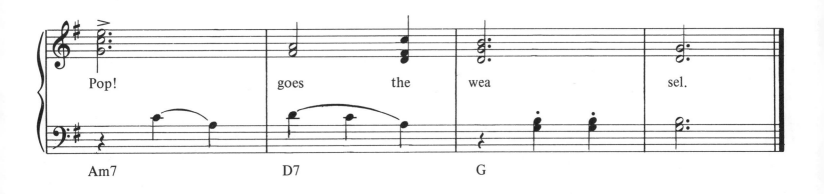

© Copyright 1984 Dorsey Brothers Music Limited, London W1.

Oh Where Has My Little Dog Gone

Traditional

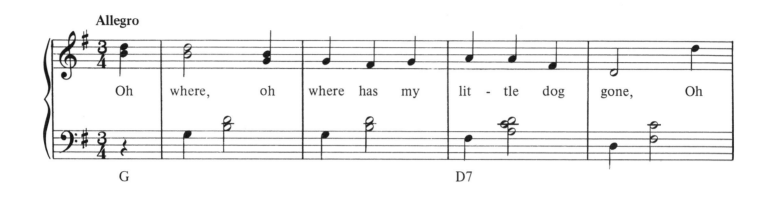

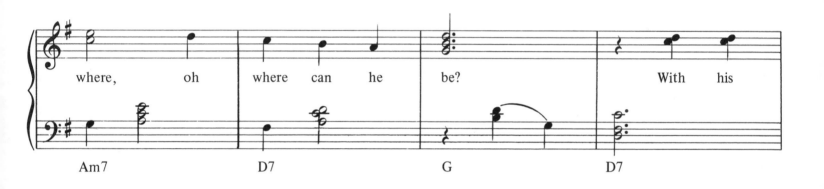

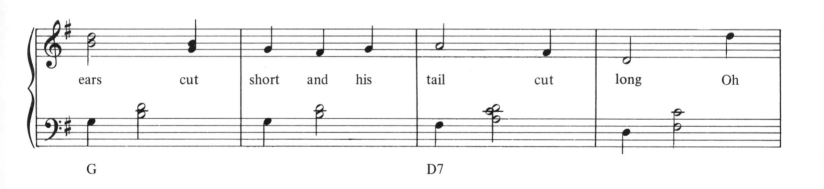

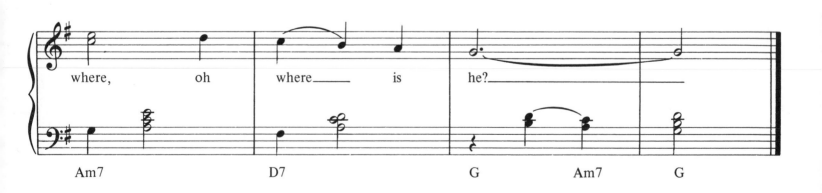

© Copyright 1984 Dorsey Brothers Music Limited, London W1.

Baa Baa Black Sheep

Traditional

Baa, Baa black sheep have you an - y wool?

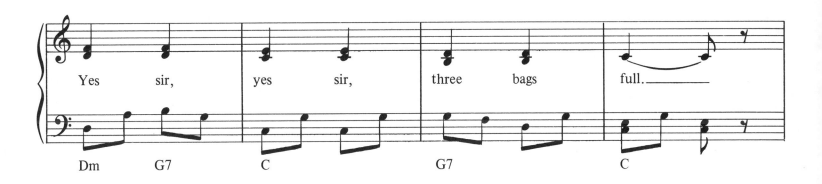

Yes sir, yes sir, three bags full._____

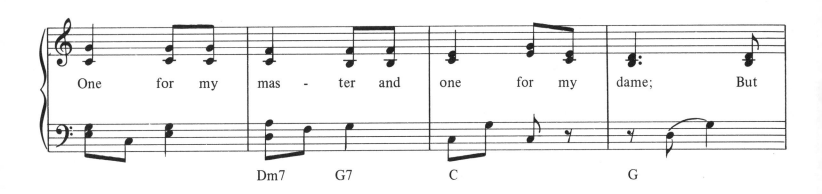

One for my mas - ter and one for my dame; But

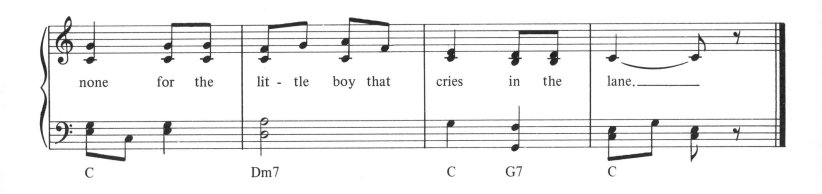

none for the lit - tle boy that cries in the lane._____

© Copyright 1984 Dorsey Brothers Music Limited, London W1.

11

Hickory Dickory Dock

Traditional

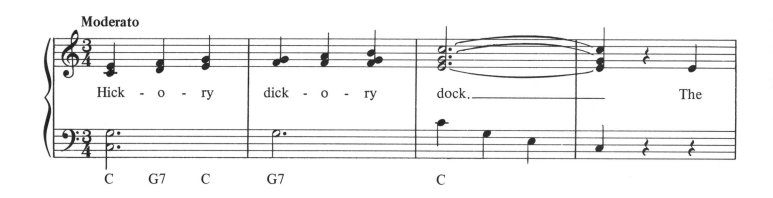

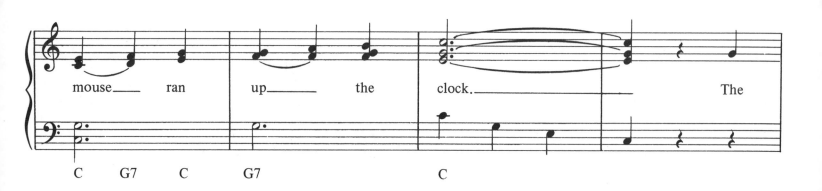

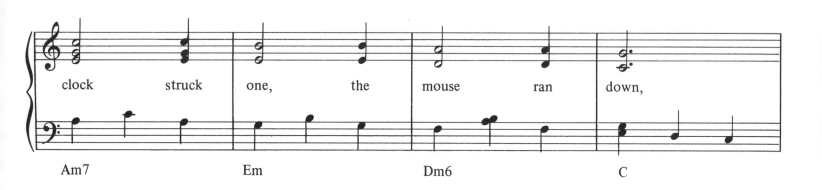

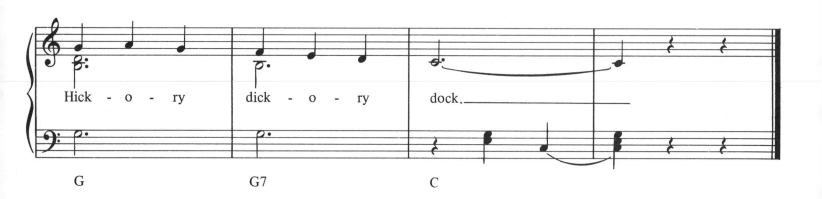

© Copyright 1984 Dorsey Brothers Music Limited, London W1.

Here We Go Gathering Nuts In May

Traditional

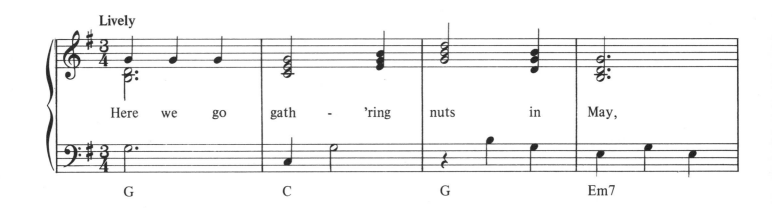

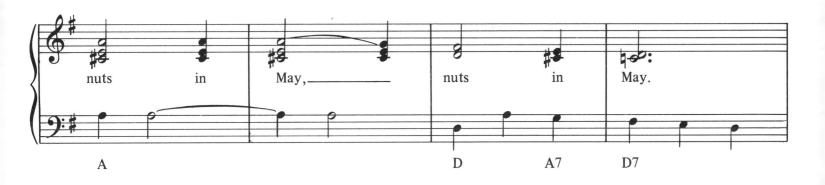

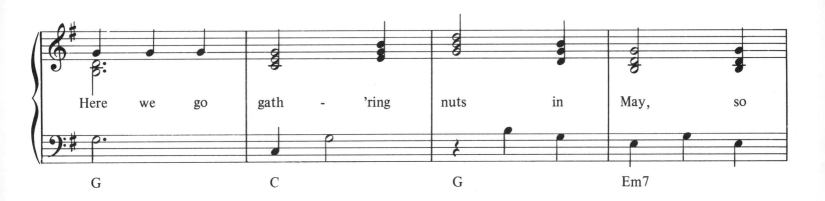

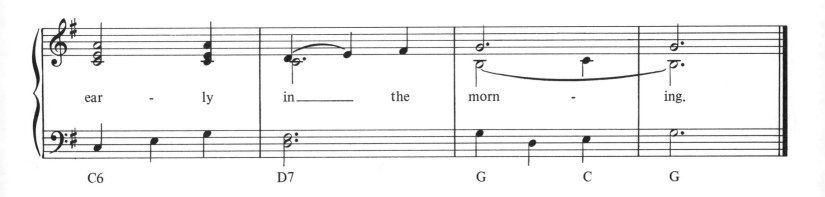

© Copyright 1984 Dorsey Brothers Music Limited, London W1.

Humpty Dumpty

Traditional

Allegro

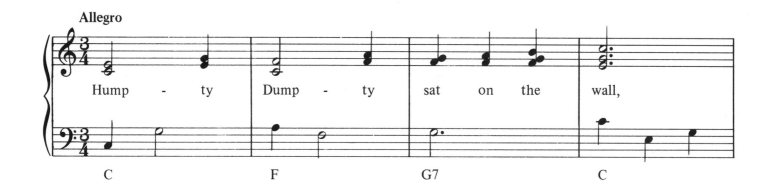

Hump - ty Dump - ty sat on the wall,

C F G7 C

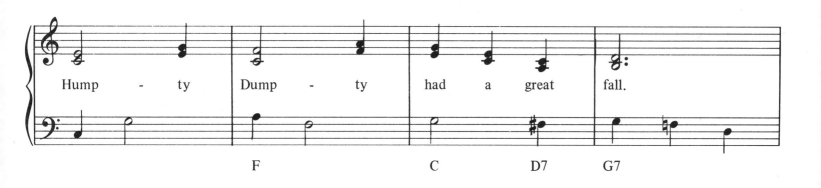

Hump - ty Dump - ty had a great fall.

F C D7 G7

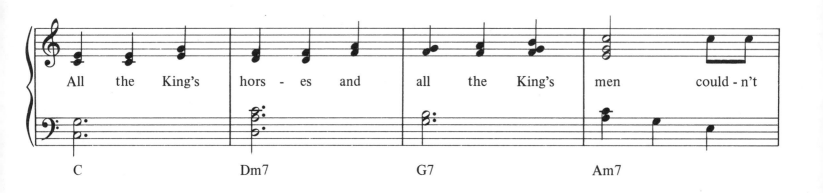

All the King's hors - es and all the King's men could - n't

C Dm7 G7 Am7

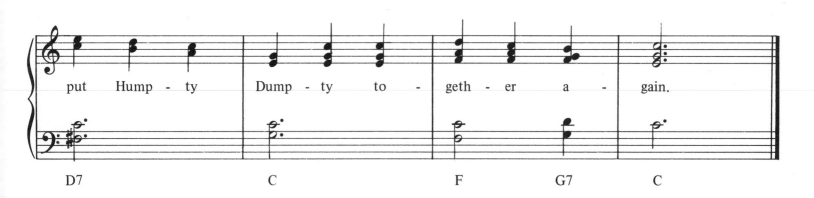

put Hump - ty Dump - ty to - geth - er a - gain.

D7 C F G7 C

© Copyright 1984 Dorsey Brothers Music Limited, London W1.

Three Blind Mice

Traditional

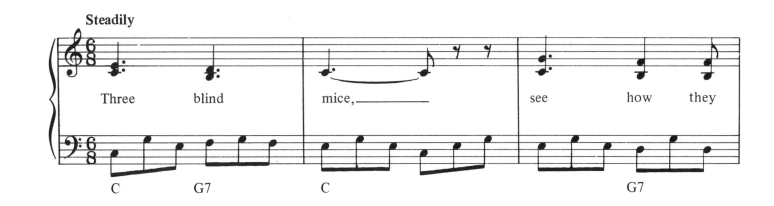

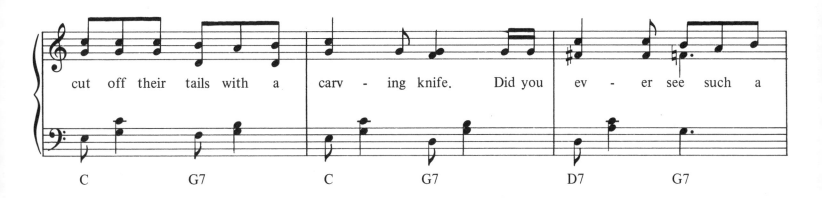

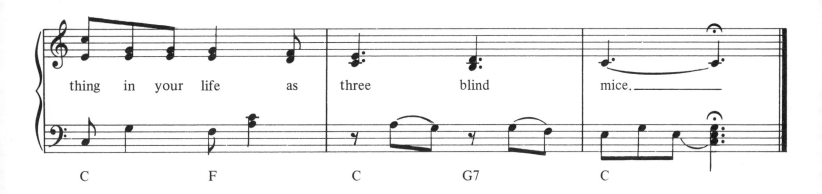

© Copyright 1984 Dorsey Brothers Music Limited, London W1.

Goosey Goosey Gander

Traditional

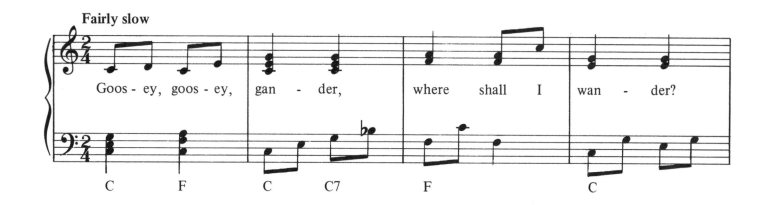

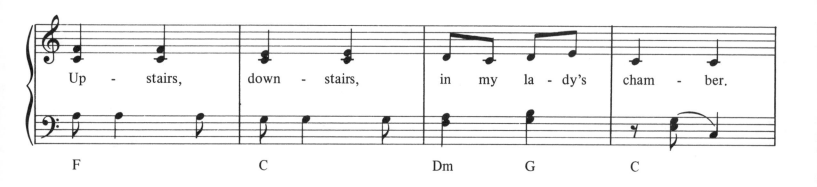

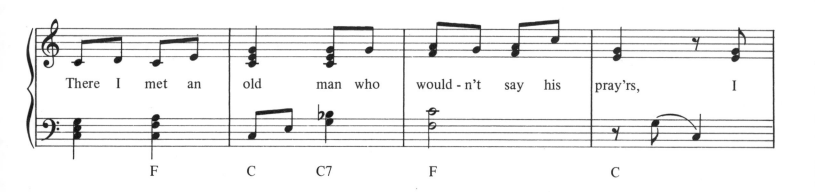

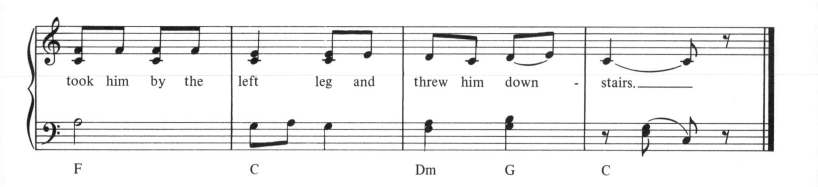

© Copyright 1984 Dorsey Brothers Music Limited, London W1.

Hey Diddle Diddle

Traditional

Moderato

Hey did - dle did - dle, the cat and the fid - dle, the

F   C7 Bb C7   F   C7 Bb C7

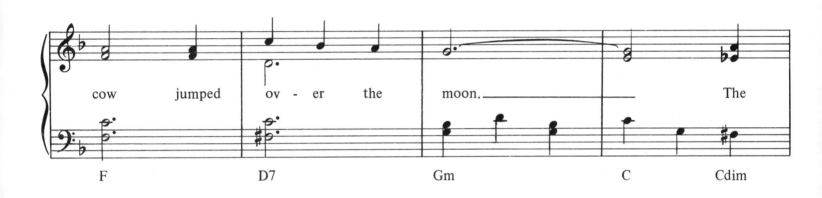

cow jumped ov - er the moon._____ The

F   D7   Gm   C Cdim

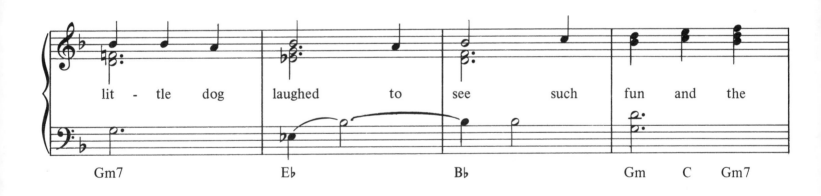

lit - tle dog laughed to see such fun and the

Gm7   Eb   Bb   Gm C Gm7

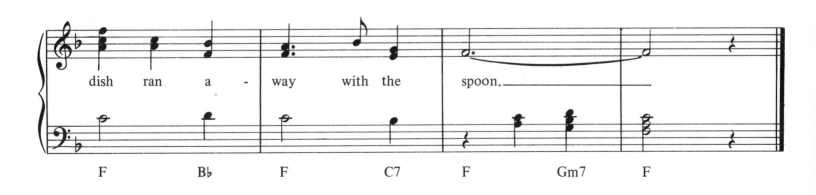

dish ran a - way with the spoon._____

F Bb   F C7   F Gm7   F

© Copyright 1984 Dorsey Brothers Music Limited, London W1.

Here We Go Round
The Mulberry Bush

Traditional

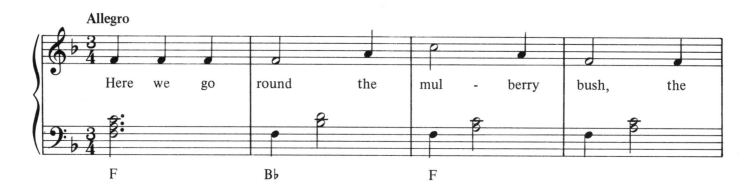

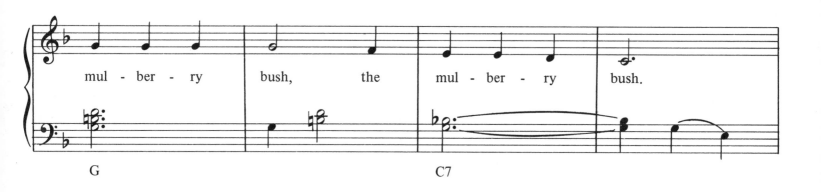

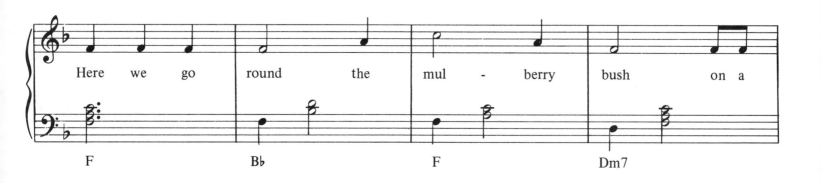

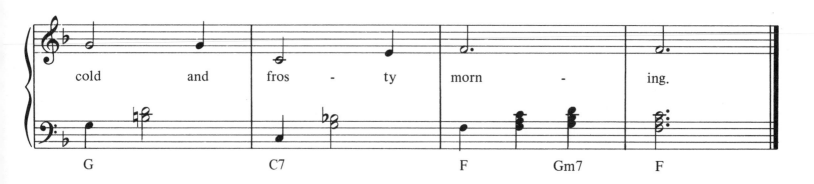

© Copyright 1984 Dorsey Brothers Music Limited, London W1.

Ding Dong Bell

Traditional

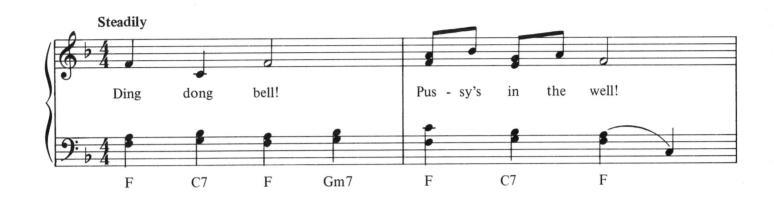

© Copyright 1984 Dorsey Brothers Music Limited, London W1.

Polly Put The Kettle On

Traditional

Moderato

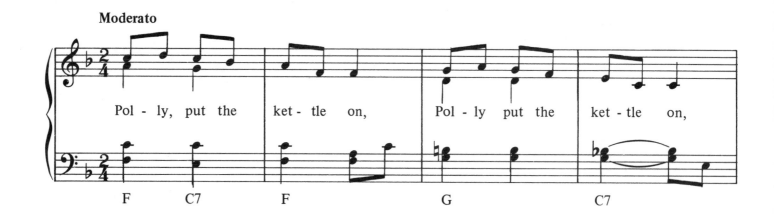

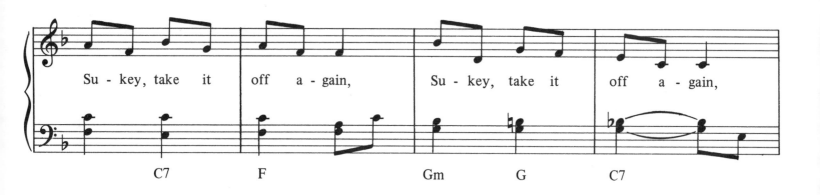

20

© Copyright 1984 Dorsey Brothers Music Limited, London W1.

Girls And Boys Come Out To Play

Traditional

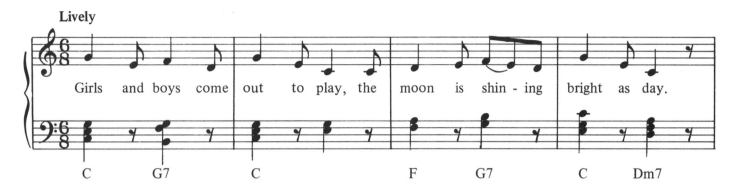

Girls and boys come out to play, the moon is shin-ing bright as day.

C　G7　C　F　G7　C　Dm7

Leave your sup-per and leave your sleep and join your play-fel-lows in the street.

C　G7　C　F　G7　C

© Copyright 1984 Dorsey Brothers Music Limited, London W1.

Pussy Cat, Pussy Cat

Traditional

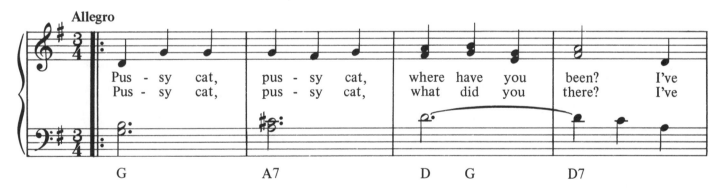

Pus-sy cat, pus-sy cat, where have you been? I've
Pus-sy cat, pus-sy cat, what did you there? I've

G　A7　D　G　D7

been up to Lon-don to look at the Queen.
fright-ened a lit-tle mouse un-der her chair.

C　D7　G　G

© Copyright 1984 Dorsey Brothers Music Limited, London W1.

Pat-A-Cake, Pat-A Cake
Baker's Man

Traditional

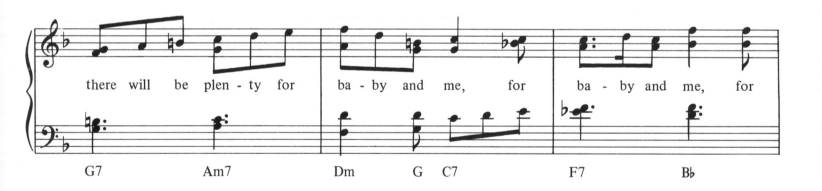

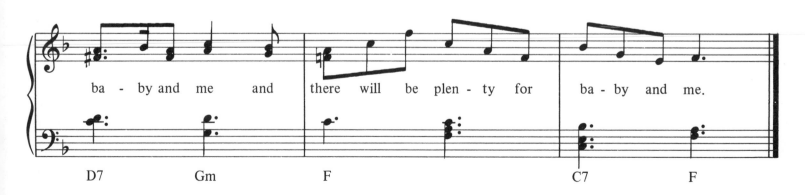

© Copyright 1984 Dorsey Brothers Music Limited, London W1.

Jack And Jill

Traditional

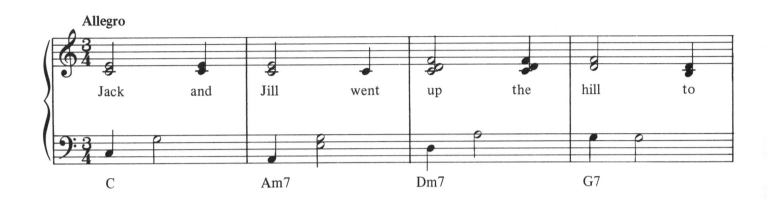

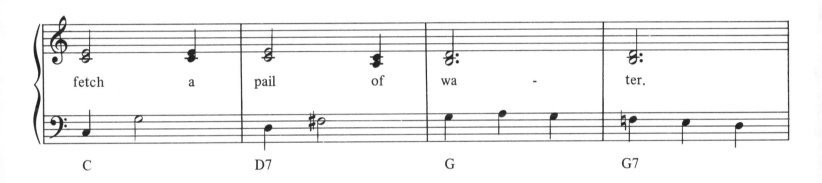

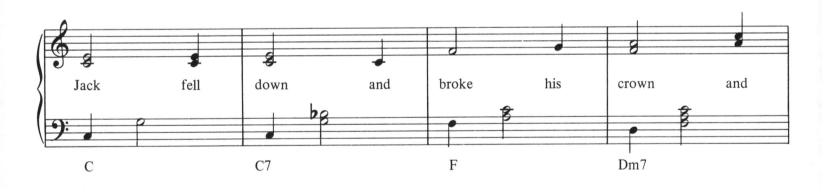

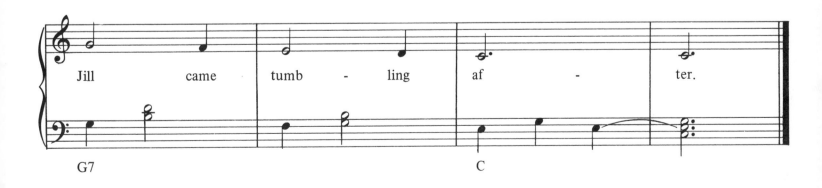

© Copyright 1984 Dorsey Brothers Music Limited, London W1.

There Was An Old Man

Traditional

Moderato

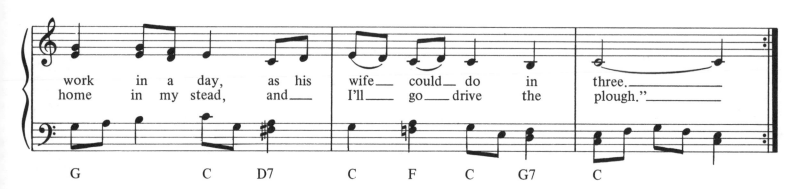

3. "But you must milk the Tidy cow,
    For fear that she go dry;
    And you must feed the little pigs
    That are within the stye.

4. And you must mind the speckled hen
    For fear she lay away;
    And you must reel the spool of yarn
    That I spun yesterday."

5. The old woman took a staff in her hand
    And went to drive the plough;
    The old man took a pail in his hand,
    And went to milk the cow.

6. But Tidy hinched and Tidy flinched,
    And Tidy broke his nose;
    And Tidy gave him such a blow
    That the blood ran down to his toes.

7. "Hi! Tidy! ho! Tidy! high!
    Tidy, do stand still!
    If ever I milk you, Tidy, again,
    'Twill be sore against my will."

© Copyright 1984 Dorsey Brothers Music Limited, London W1.

Diddle Diddle Dumpling, My Son John

Traditional

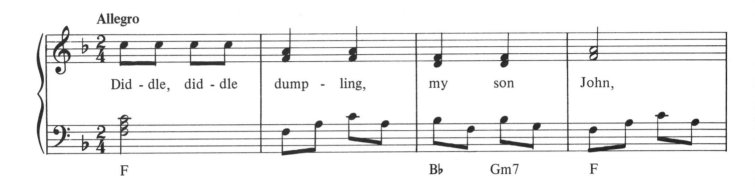

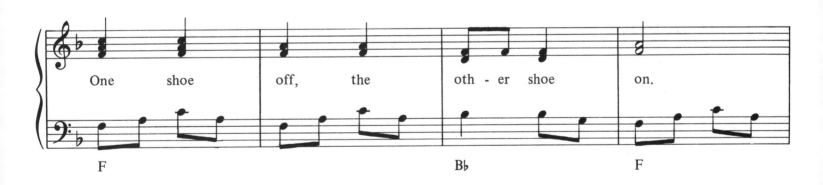

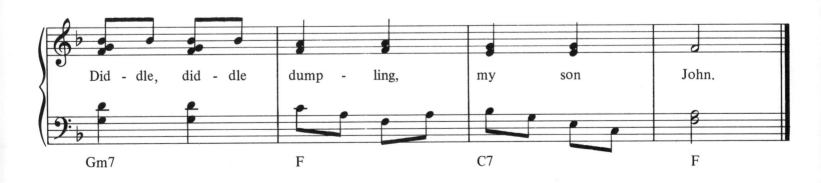

© Copyright 1984 Dorsey Brothers Music Limited, London W1.

25

Simple Simon

Traditional

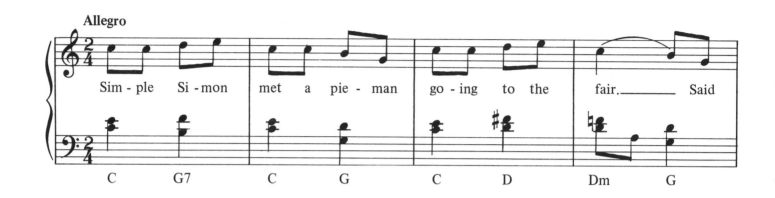

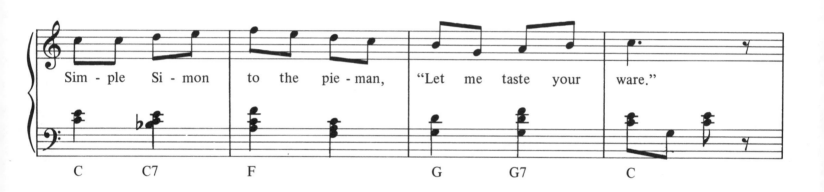

© Copyright 1984 Dorsey Brothers Music Limited, London W1.

I Love Little Pussy

Traditional

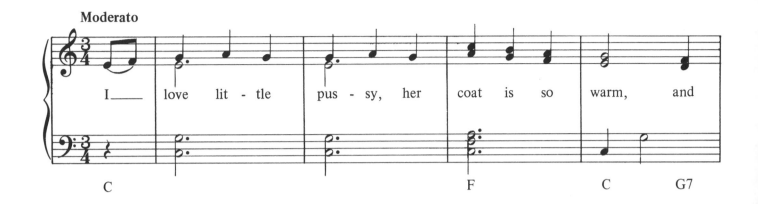

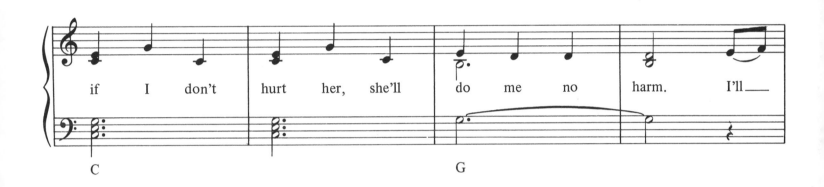

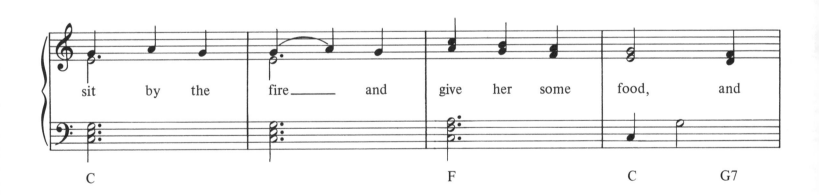

© Copyright 1984 Dorsey Brothers Music Limited, London W1.

Twinkle Twinkle Little Star

Traditional

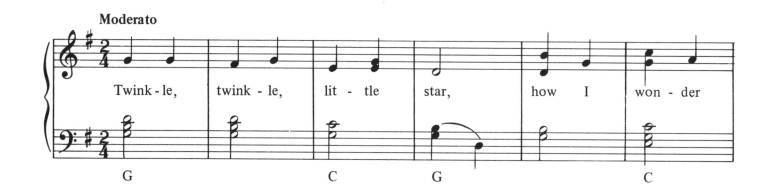

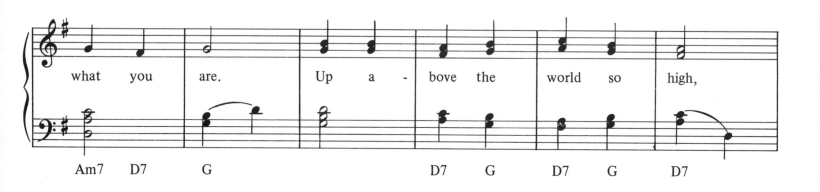

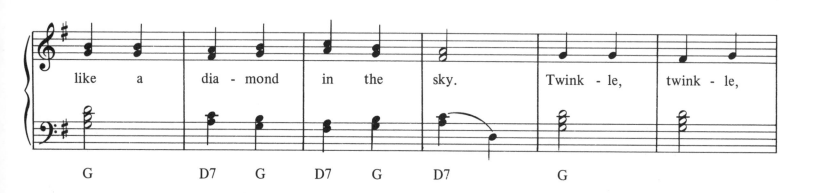

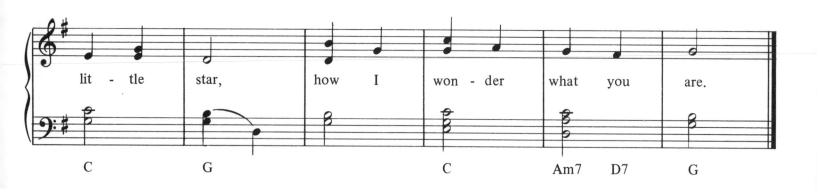

© Copyright 1984 Dorsey Brothers Music Limited, London W1.

Little Miss Muffet

Traditional

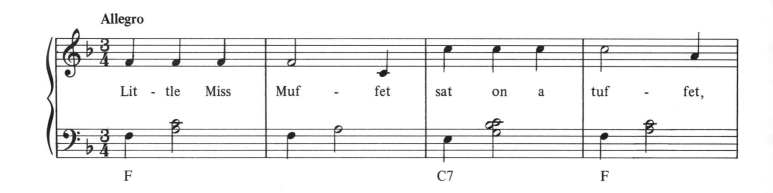

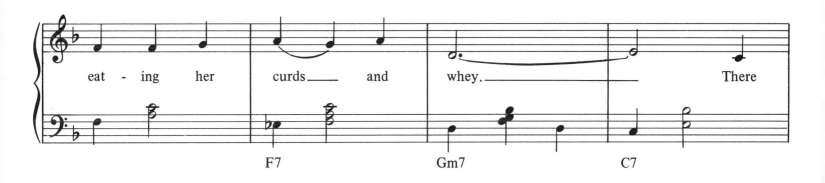

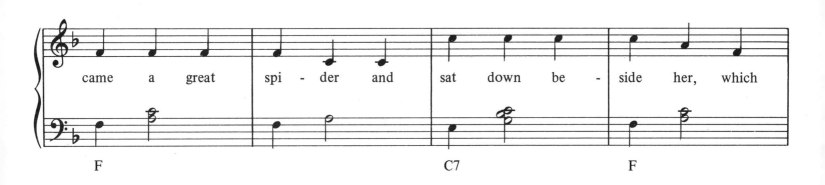

© Copyright 1984 Dorsey Brothers Music Limited, London W1.

Old Mother Hubbard

Traditional

Old Moth-er Hub-bard, she went to the cup-board to

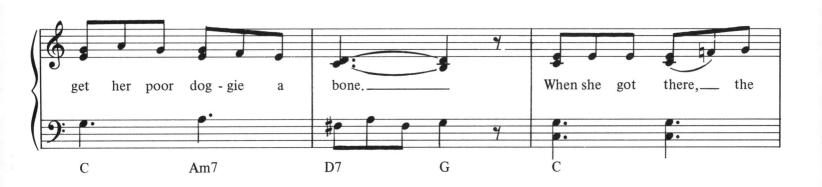

get her poor dog-gie a bone._____ When she got there,___ the

cup-board was bare___ and so the poor dog-gie got none._____ She___

went to the ba-kers' to buy him some bread___ but when she came back, the poor

© Copyright 1984 Dorsey Brothers Music Limited, London W1.

dog - gie was dead. She— went to the join-er's to buy him a cof-fin and

D7   G   C   F

when she came back—— the dog - gie was laugh - ing. She—

C   G7   C

went to the butch-er's to get him some tripe—— and when she came back he was

       F   C   Am7

smok-ing a pipe. She— went to the fish shop to buy him some fish—— and

D7   G   C   F

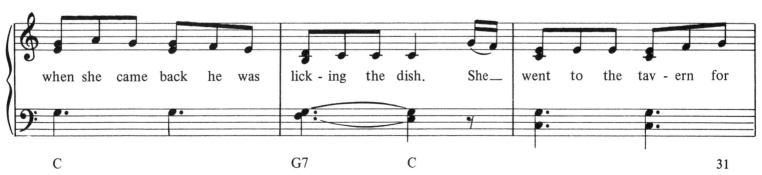

when she came back he was lick - ing the dish. She— went to the tav - ern for

C   G7   C

white wine and red___ and   when she came back dog-gie   stood on his head. She___

F   C   Am7   D7   G

went to the hat-ter's to   buy him a hat___ and   when she came back he was

C   F   G

feed-ing the cat. She___   went to the tai-lor's to   buy him a coat___ and

G7   C   F

when she came back he was   rid-ing the goat. She___   went to the bar-ber's to

C   Am7   D7   G   C

buy him a wig___ and   when she came back he was   danc-ing a jig. She___

F   C   G7   C

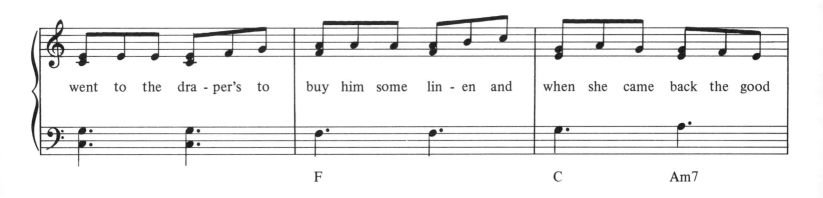

went to the dra - per's to | buy him some lin - en and | when she came back the good

F | C   Am7

dog was a spin - ning, She | went to the hos - ier's to | buy him some hose___ and

Dm   G7 | C | F

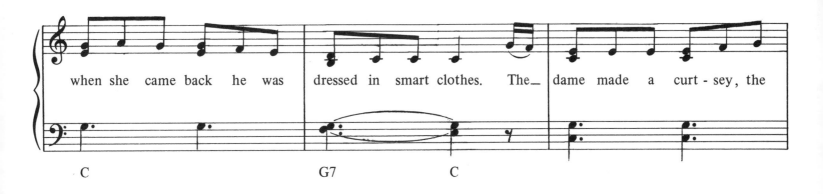

when she came back he was | dressed in smart clothes. The___ | dame made a curt - sey, the

C | G7   C |

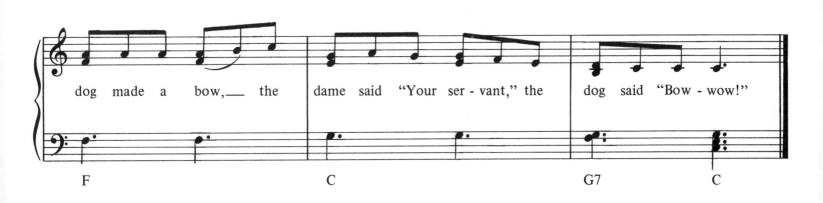

dog made a bow,___ the | dame said "Your ser - vant," the | dog said "Bow - wow!"

F | C | G7   C

33

Ride A Cock Horse

Traditional

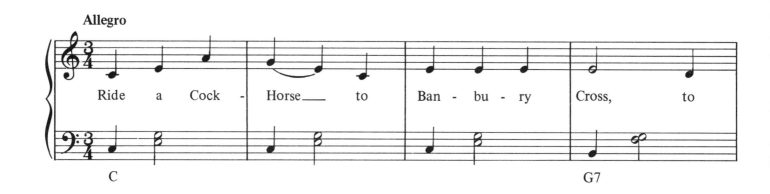

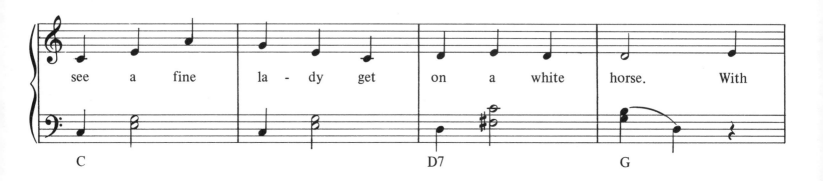

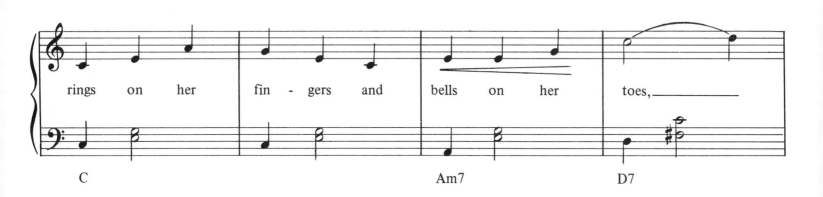

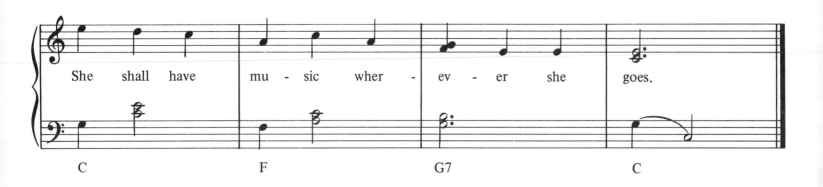

© Copyright 1984 Dorsey Brothers Music Limited, London W1.

Little Tommy Tucker

Traditional

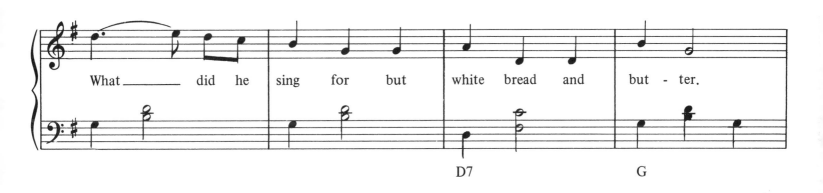

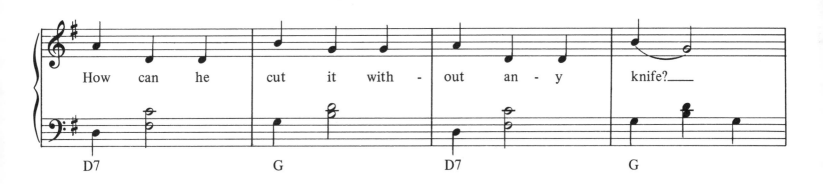

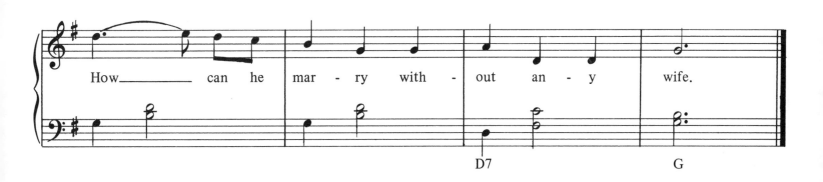

© Copyright 1984 Dorsey Brothers Music Limited, London W1.

Georgie Porgie

Traditional

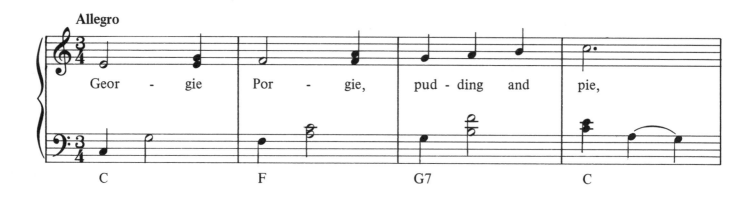

Geor - gie Por - gie, pud - ding and pie,

C   F   G7   C

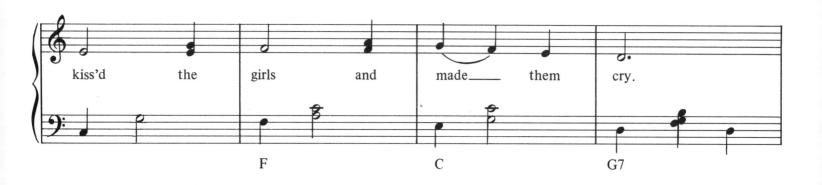

kiss'd the girls and made___ them cry.

F   C   G7

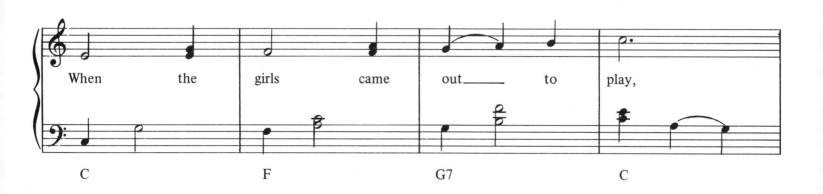

When the girls came out___ to play,

C   F   G7   C

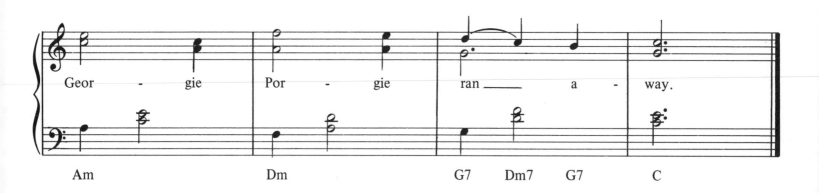

Geor - gie Por - gie ran ___ a - way.

Am   Dm   G7 Dm7 G7   C

© Copyright 1984 Dorsey Brothers Music Limited, London W1.

The Grand Old Duke Of York

Traditional

In march tempo

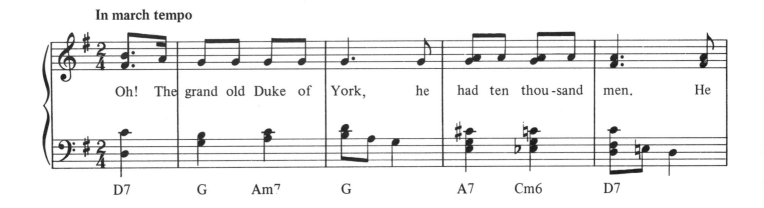

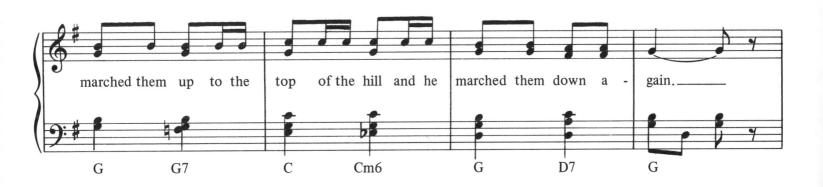

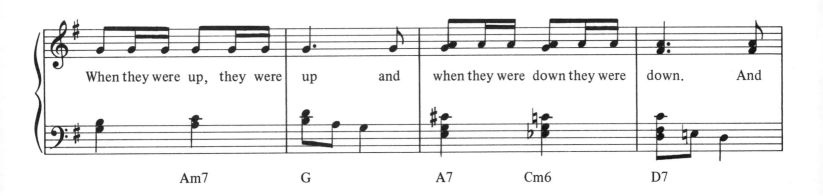

© Copyright 1984 Dorsey Brothers Music Limited, London W1.

The Farmer's In His Den

Traditional

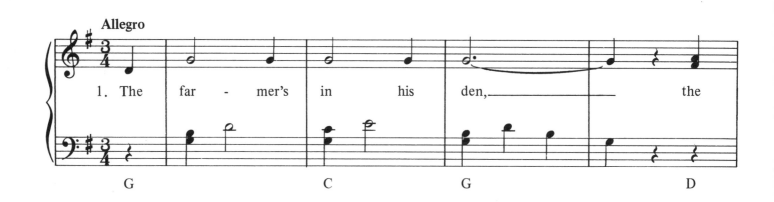

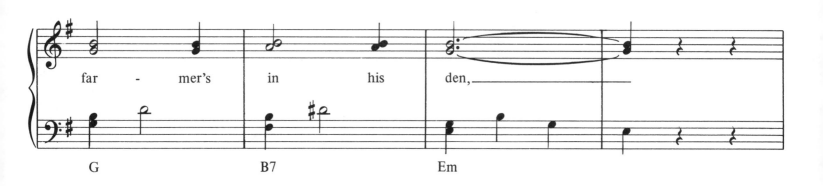

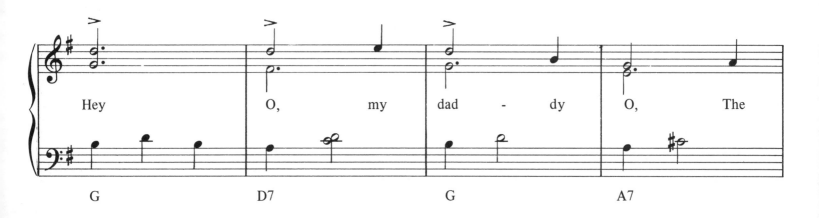

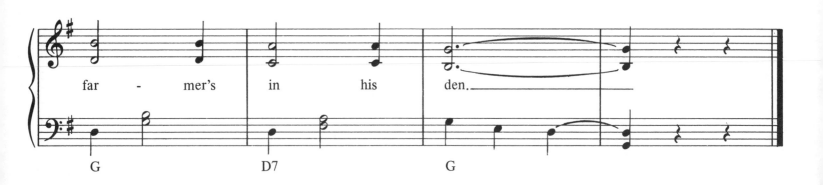

© Copyright 1984 Dorsey Brothers Music Limited, London W1.

Verse 2. The farmer wants a wife,
The farmer wants a wife,
Hey O etc.

3. The wife wants a child,
The wife wants a child,
Hey O etc.

4. The child wants a nurse,
The child wants a nurse,
Hey O etc.

5. The nurse wants a dog,
The nurse wants a dog,
Hey O etc.

6. The dog wants a bone,
The dog wants a bone,
Hey O etc.

7. We all clap the dog,
We all clap the dog,
Hey O etc.

The children form a ring round the farmer and dance round while singing Verse 1. The farmer chooses a wife who takes his place in the centre of the ring while Verse 2 is sung. The wife chooses a child; the child chooses a nurse; and so on until the last verse when the players adopt actions to suit the words "clap the dog."

There Was A Crooked Man

Traditional

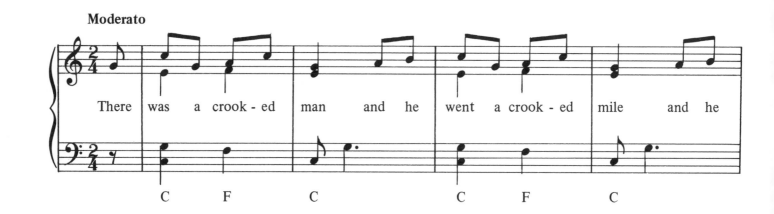

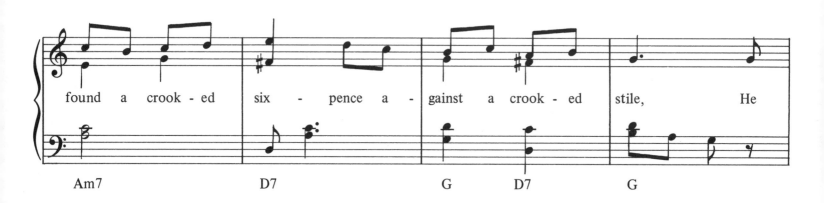

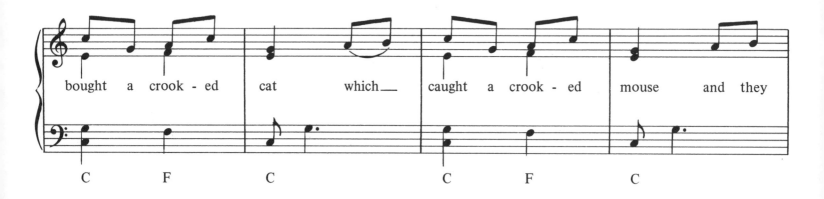

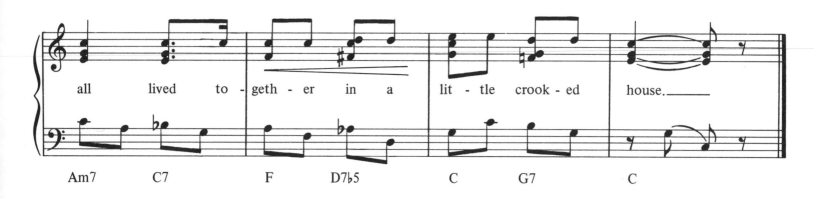

© Copyright 1984 Dorsey Brothers Music Limited, London W1.

Taffy

Traditional

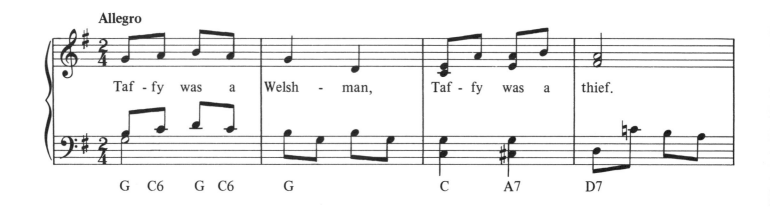

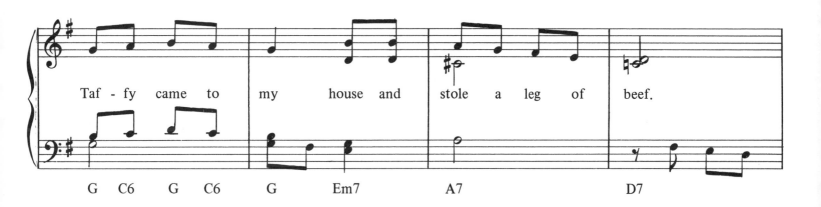

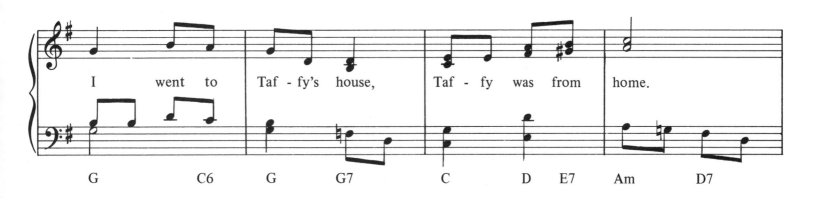

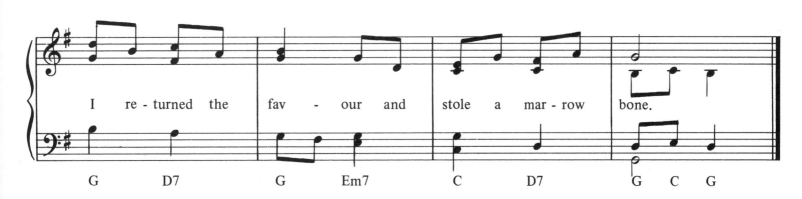

© Copyright 1984 Dorsey Brothers Music Limited, London W1.

Ring-A-Ring Of Roses

Traditional

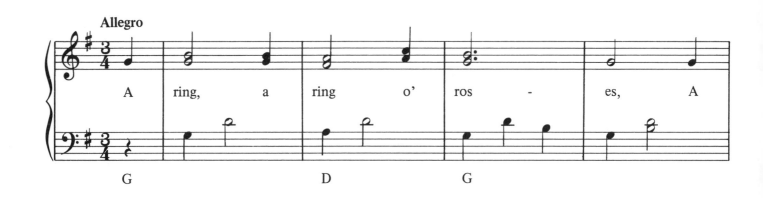

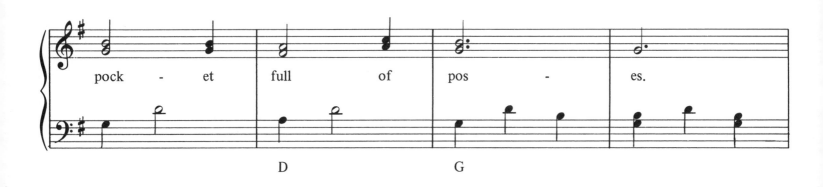

© Copyright 1984 Dorsey Brothers Music Limited, London W1.

Jingle Bells

Traditional

© Copyright 1984 Dorsey Brothers Music Limited, London W1.

Where Are You Going To My Pretty Maid

Traditional

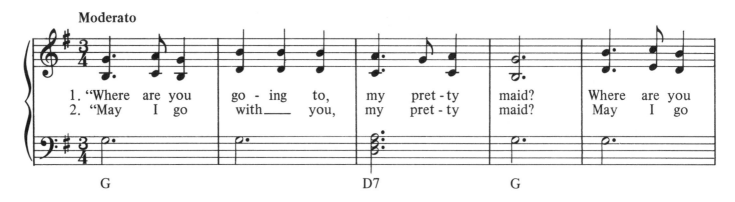

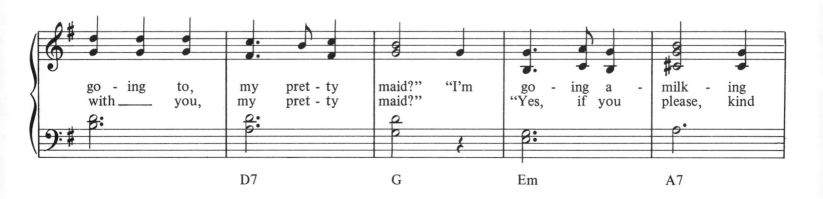

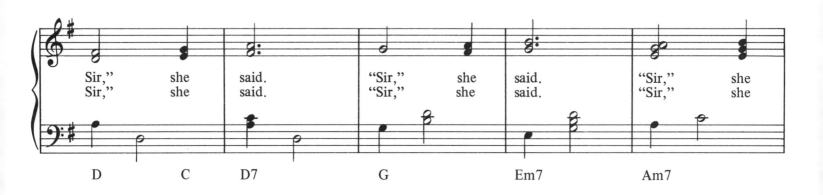

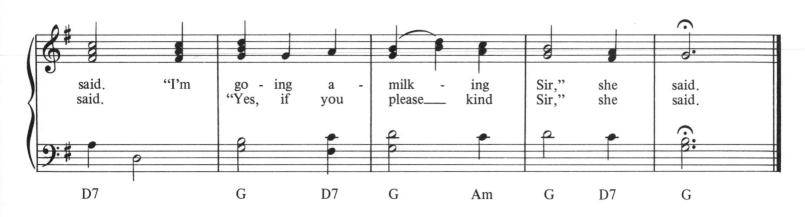

© Copyright 1984 Dorsey Brothers Music Limited, London W1.

Mary Had A Little Lamb

Traditional

Moderato

© Copyright 1984 Dorsey Brothers Music Limited, London W1.

Hark Hark The Dogs Do Bark

Traditional

Allegro

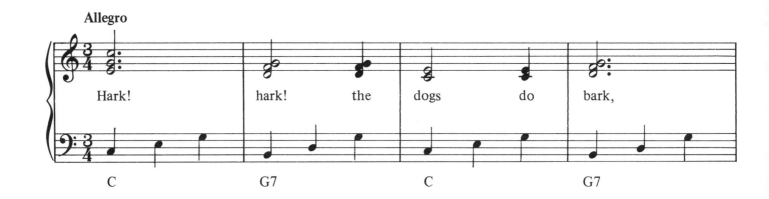

Hark! hark! the dogs do bark,

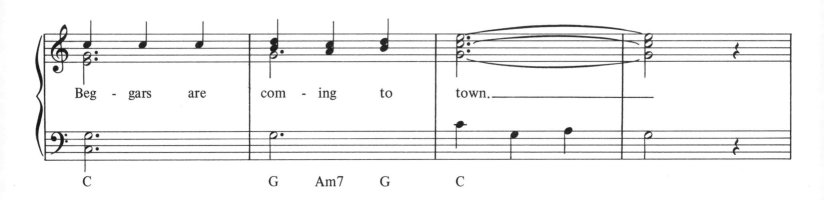

Beg - gars are com - ing to town.

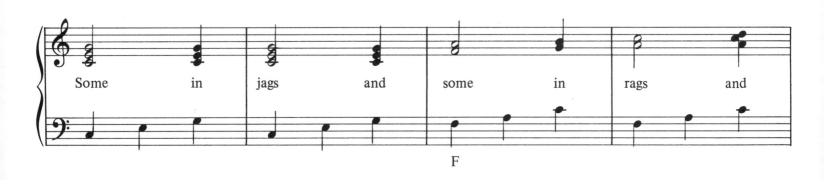

Some in jags and some in rags and

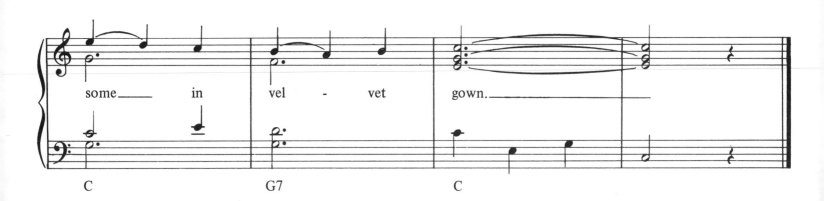

some in vel - vet gown.

© Copyright 1984 Dorsey Brothers Music Limited, London W1.

Hot Cross Buns

Traditional

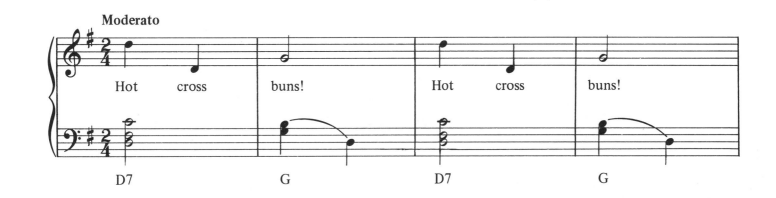

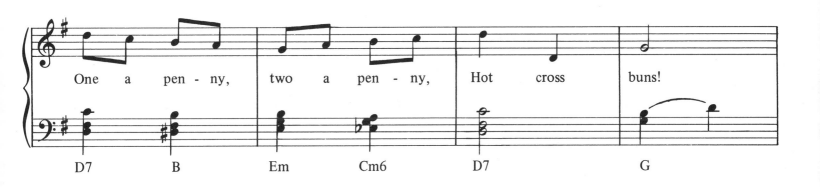

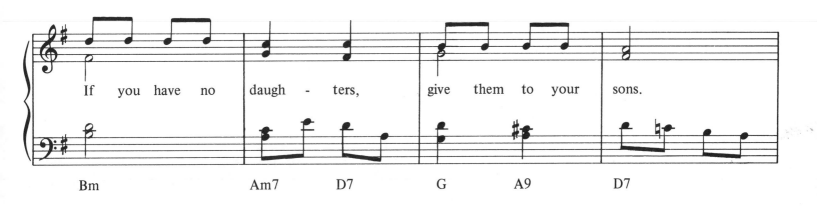

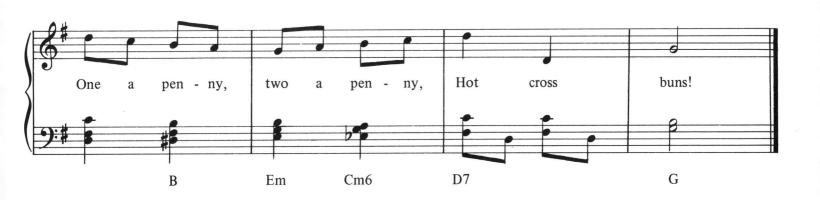

© Copyright 1984 Dorsey Brothers Music Limited, London W1.

The Beatles

Enya

Phil Collins

Van Morrison

Bob Dylan

Sting

Paul Simon

Tracy Chapman

Eric Clapton

Pink Floyd

New Kids On The Block

Bringing you the
words

**All the latest in rock and pop.
Plus the brightest and best in West
End show scores. Music books for
every instrument under the sun.
And exciting new teach-yourself
ideas like "Let's Play Keyboard" -
in cassette/book packs, or on video.
Available from all good music shops.**

Bryan Adams

Tina Turner

Elton John

and

Bee Gees

Whitney Houston

AC/DC

music

**Music Sales' complete
catalogue lists thousands of
titles and is available free
from your local music shop,
or direct from Music Sales
Limited. Please send a
cheque or postal order for
£1.50 (for postage) to:**

Music Sales Limited
Newmarket Road,
Bury St Edmunds,
Suffolk IP33 3YB

Buddy

Five Guys Named Moe

Les Misérables

West Side Story

Phantom Of The Opera

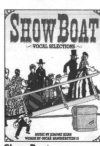
Show Boat

The Rocky Horror Show

**Bringing you the
world's best music.**